I0447626

Police Personality and Domestic Violence

A Forensic Psychological
Approach

Police Personality and

Domestic Violence

A Forensic Psychological Approach

Written by Author Victoria Hargan

Copyright © 2012

For permission requests, write or email to the publisher, addressed
below.

Amazon CreateSpace
4900 LaCross Road
North Charleston, SC 29406
USA
Email: PolicePersonalityDV@gmail.com

Overview

Domestic violence by police officers is a complex phenomenon and remains a problem to members of law enforcement, the criminal justice system and to the medical and mental health communities. The author reviews a historical look at police culture, police training, and dynamics of domestic violence as they relate to police personality and domestic violence. This book compares personality traits and characteristics of domestic abusers to the police personality to determine whether police officers are predisposed to domestic violence. It is suggested that police personality traits and characteristics resemble those of domestic abusers. It is further suggested that these traits make effective police officers. The lack of policies in place in addition to the absence of enforcement of laws and policies within the police agency has made domestic violence among law enforcement difficult to challenge, treat, and resolve. The author offers suggestions to reduce and eliminate domestic violence by police officers.

Police Personality and Domestic Violence

Table of Contents

Chapter One

Defining Domestic Violence by Police Officers

Domestic violence is a complex and multifaceted phenomenon. It remains a global issue that continues to be reported in epidemic proportion. Researchers have endlessly researched domestic violence in many ways: causation of domestic violence, dynamics of domestic violence, scope of the problem, the cycle of violence, the power imbalance between victim and batterer, the impact that domestic violence has on society as a whole; including statistics, cost of health care from injuries sustained by the victim (including mental health services), and rehabilitation for the offender, among other penalties. After decades of research, domestic violence remains a global issue.

Domestic violence by police officers is yet another area of study and is considered a sub-population of abuse. What

Police Personality and Domestic Violence

does that mean? With domestic violence being the general term for domestic violence, police perpetrated domestic violence (PPDV) is another term utilized to describe a culture who engages in domestic violence. In this book we will examine the police culture and police officers who perpetrate domestic violence.

Police perpetrated domestic violence (PPDV) is defined as domestic violence perpetrated by a law enforcement officer. The International Association of Chiefs of Police (IACP) defines domestic violence by police officers as follows: "Domestic violence" refers to an act or pattern of violence perpetrated by a police officer upon his or her intimate partner not done in defense of self or others, including but not limited to the following: Bodily injury or threat of imminent bodily injury, Sexual battery, Physical restraint, Property crime directed at the victim, Stalking, Violation of a court order of protection or similar injunction, Death threats or death " (IACP 2002).

Further, the IACP defines an intimate partner as "An intimate partner" of a police officer is any person who meets one or more of the following criteria: Is or was legally married to the police officer, Has a child in common with the police officer, Has or had a dating relationship with the police officer, Is specified as an intimate partner by state law, Is cohabitating or has cohabitated romantically with the police officer.

Police Personality and Domestic Violence

Domestic violence perpetrated by law enforcement is considered a sub-population of domestic abusers which contains cultural factors within the police culture.

Statistics

Domestic violence by police officers continues to remain a health issue among police families and victims; and PPDV remains a problem within the law enforcement community. The psychology profession and research arena have struggled to provide interventions and strategies due to lack of cooperation by law enforcement agencies, and lack of evidenced based practice and empirical studies related to the police culture in relationship to domestic violence. "Researchers have established that law enforcement officers consistently report using violence with their intimate partners, although the reported rates have varied. Klein and Klein (2000) found rates lower than that of the general population – around 5% – while other studies found much higher rates, up to 40% (Neidig, Russell, & Seng, 1992). Feder found 24% in 1997; Ryan found 10% in 2000; Gershon found 9% in 2000; and Johnson found 40% in 1991. While no precise rate of officer-involved domestic violence has been formally established, it is clear that officer-involved domestic violence exists and deserves careful attention (IACP, 2003b)" (Oehme & Martin, 2011).

Police Personality and Domestic Violence

Research has revealed that domestic violence by the general population is underreported and domestic violence by police officers is believed to lack sufficient statistical data partially due to the police policing themselves; thus, resulting in lack of data, and altered results as to how many police officers engage in domestic violence. When a police officer is charged with domestic violence, the administration of the police department and Internal Affairs investigate the incident. Many times, the department attempts to resolve the issue internally. This means that the police department may contact the victim, interview the victim, and tell the victim that they will handle it without going through the typical channels that a victim would normally go through if the perpetrator was not a police officer.

Furthermore, another complaint among victims includes not receiving an official or formal complaint number. This is because the police report is not available in the records department and remains part of the individual officer's personal file. This can leave the victim vulnerable with lack of supporting documentation. When a victim goes to file for a personal protection order (PPO), supported documentation is essential. This is only one reason why documentation is vital.

The department will contact the officer involved in the DV incident and will remind the officer of professional

Police Personality and Domestic Violence

conduct both on and off the job. The administration will often leave the officer with a warning and the officer who engaged in DV leaves the victim with a warning of their own (Not to call the department to report DV) and the violence escalates for the victim. The lack of responsibility by the department, the lack of accountability by the officer, in addition *to lack of punishment* imposed on the officer puts the victim, society and the law enforcement community in a dangerous and precarious position.

A very important and powerful variable that may be partially responsible for the *"lack of's"* is the federal law that may threaten the officer's job when charging the officer. The Lautenberg Amendment to the control gun control act (1968), family violence act states that anyone convicted of domestic violence cannot carry a firearm. This puts the police officer in a precarious position since part of the officer's tools includes a firearm.

Chapter Two

Domestic Violence a Historical View

Police personality has been an interest to psychologists for decades; however, police psychology was not recognized as a formal discipline until the late 1970's and early 1980's; with police brutality at the forefront of interest to psychologists. Psychologists were interested in why some police officers abused citizens whereas other officers did not. Another interest to psychologists was how police work affected the police officer's overall well-being, including physical and mental health and family conflict.

There was very little interest in domestic violence within the police family during that era since domestic violence was considered "a private family matter" and was expected to be kept a secret and was commonplace among families. The old adage "The rule of thumb" was a rule followed centuries previous that a man could use a switch on his wife no bigger than his thumb; and was a way to protect the wife.

It wasn't until the feminine movement began to emerge during the 1970's that caught the attention of the criminal justice system, medical and mental health fields. In fact, "Until 1976, rape laws in all 50 states contained a Marital Rape Exemption specifically to prevent husbands who raped their wives from being charged with a crime" (RAINN, 2009). In addition, it wasn't until 1996 that marital rape was abolished as even being a crime. This meant that a man could legally rape his wife and it was considered a wife's marital responsibility to have sex with him when and if he wanted to engage in sexual activity. This is disturbing and reveals how very little domestic violence; including marital rape has evolved over the years. Police family violence is considered a sub-population of abuse where culture changes the outcome for the victim.

Domestic violence perpetrated by law enforcement is a foreign area of study for the scholarly arena. The limited research available on this topic has revealed that police officers possess many of the same personality traits that domestic abusers possess such as authoritarianism, coercion, manipulation, deception, psychological tactics, isolation, high rates of substance abuse, relationship issues, and a sense of entitlement are examples. Police training adds to the complexity, power imbalance and overall dynamics within the

Police Personality and Domestic Violence

individual officer's relationship.

Additionally, police officers are trained to control and subdue crowds and individuals. It is suggested that police training, tactics, techniques, in addition to police personality traits further enhance domestic violence within the police family. Police officers learn to control situations during training, and it takes a firm, assertive, authoritative demeanor to gain control over a person or situation. Police training skills used on the streets are often carried over into the home causing conflict and arguments, potentially resulting in domestic violence. "The competitive and controlling nature of many police officers leads them to want to win arguments rather than resolve problems" (Nicoletti & Spencer-Thomas, 2000).

Police Personality and Domestic Violence

Chapter Three

The Police Personality

Personality Theory and Development

Research has shown that personality development is a result of multiple factors, and one theory is neither right or wrong in identifying how and why people develop certain personality traits. Foundational theorists such as Piaget, known for cognitive development; Freud's psychosocial development theory, in addition to Freud's Structural Model of Personality; Erikson's Stages of Psychosocial Development and Kohlberg's Stages of Moral Development; and Nature versus Nurture debate all provide well-formulated theories of personality development; however, it is an integrated theory that possess a better explanation for one's personality and behavioral traits.

Integrated theoretical causes include a person's biopsychosocial makeup and development to be responsible for personality development. This includes individual life circumstances, experiences, genetics, environment, socioeconomic status, educational status, physical health, mental health, disability, cultural influence, race, gender, creed, religion, and occupational influence that are responsible for the way people think, decisions they make, how they feel and perceive the world and choice of lifestyle. "Occupational environments can influence and shape perceptions and interpretations of events and situations" (Skolnick). It is suggested that individual personality traits along with police training constitutes the "Police Personality." "Insight into the occupational environment of police officers can help to provide a more complete understanding of officer behavior and decision- making" (Skolnick).

Police Personality

Personality structure among police officers is better understood when applying an integrated theoretical approach to personality. Personality has been described to varying degrees in the literature. I have provided definitions of personality defined: "Personality is the entire mental organization of a human being at any stage of his development. It embraces every phase of human character: intellect, temperament, skill, morality, and every attitude that has been built up in the course of one's life" (Warren & Carmichael, 1930, p. 333).

A second definition of personality is described as: "An

Police Personality and Domestic Violence

individual's pattern of psychological processes arising from motives, feelings, thoughts, and other major areas of psychological function. Personality is expressed through its influences on the body, in conscious mental life, and through the individual's social behavior" (Mayer, 2005).

Personality includes a person's thoughts, feelings and behaviors to which make an individual unique. There are components of personality that pertain to all populations which include consistency, behaviors, thoughts feelings stimulated by psychological and physiological processes. For example, individuals possess consistent behaviors and traits across most situations. Additionally, it is suggested that our personality is a psychological phenomenon that occurs psychologically; and this phenomenon is influenced by a physiological response that effects how we respond to environmental stimuli.

Furthermore, personality is not only seen in behavior, it is also evident in how we think, what we feel and how we engage in our personal and professional relationships and socialization.

Police Personality Traits

Understanding basic concepts relating to personality will help to identify police personality and whether certain personality traits are responsible for the high rate of domestic violence within law enforcement. Typical personality traits possessed by police officers include authoritative, suspiciousness, aggressive, assertive, dominance, conservative, isolation, entitlement, manipulative, deception, risk taking, thrill seeking, controlling, solidarity and cohesion among the profession to be among the most common.

Skolnick has labeled the police personality as a "working personality" of police that is influenced by police culture and environment. "The working personality of police is shaped by the need to establish one's authority, the ever-present threat of danger, and the need for efficiency. The working personality influences the behavioral responses of police officers, providing a unique way to study and understand police behavior. The isolation police experience from the public serves to strengthen police solidarity and the working personality of officers" Skolnick).

Skolnick describes the working personality as comprising of two principal variables, danger and authority resulting in a third personality variable trait suspiciousness (Skolnick). Police officers are trained to recognize "normal" in order to be able to discern situations or suspects who may be suspicious or dangerous. For example, police officers are trained to take notice of their neighborhoods where they patrol to identify and spot things that are out of the ordinary for that particular neighborhood. In addition, constantly scanning surroundings for danger and suspicious activity helps the officer to identify the potential for danger; however constant

Police Personality and Domestic Violence

hyper-vigilance can affect the police officer's overall mental well-being. Hyper- vigilance becomes habit on duty and off duty.

Another personality trait of police officer's is conservative traits. Police officers feel safe and secure with consistent behaviors and acts, because unpredictable behavior or acts can cost them their life. Without consistency and what the officer perceives as "normal" puts the officer on edge and heightens their threat of safety and security.

Moreover, Skolnick describes the fine line between friendships and isolation that often develops between police officers and ordinary citizens "A policeman's work makes him less desirable as a friend, since norms of friendship implicate others in his work. Accordingly, the element of danger isolates the policeman socially from that segment of the population which he regards as symbolically dangerous and from the conventional population with whom he identifies" (Skolnick). This belief and identification build the solidarity among law enforcement.

Additionally, authority reinforces the isolation between officer and ordinary citizens. The paradoxical personality traits of police officers may be responsible for being accused of hypocrisy due to their own risky thrill- seeking behaviors. It is suggested that the kind of person who responds well to danger is also a person who does not always uphold a high moral code.

Police Personality and Domestic Violence

Responding to danger requires risk, aggressiveness, assertiveness, deception and creativity. Living by a high moral code does not always allow for these behaviors.

Additionally, police officers are skilled at manipulation and utilizing coercion to elicit information. This may require the officer to lie to a suspect to elicit a confession for example and lying is not a trait of someone who holds a high moral standard resulting in further isolation and encourages solidarity among law enforcement.

Police Personality and Domestic Violence

Chapter Four

Police Hiring Process and Method Selection

Police training tactics begin as early as the pre-employment phase. The hiring and selection process is lengthy and rigorous. This process includes several steps. Initially candidates must possess 60 credits hours of college classes preferably in criminal justice or Associate degree in law enforcement; a relatively clean criminal background and should be in reasonably good physical condition.

The next step is applying to a police department. The candidate is scheduled for a testing day which includes a multiple-choice exam and a physical agility test (PAT) in addition to an oral board interview. If the police candidate passes the initial multiple-choice exam and the PAT the police department will perform the background check, a psychological exam (most departments), a physical exam, a polygraph exam and voice stress analysis. Once the police candidate passes all of the required tests the candidate will go on to have an oral interview with an oral interview board. It is suggested that this is the most difficult part of the selection process and has a high rate of failure of all tests combined.

Police candidates are "schooled" on the selection process and how to pass the oral interview with countless books, websites and videos available offering tips, tricks and secret to guarantee a top score on the police pre- employment exam, evaluation and selection process.

Topics such as how to dress, what to say and not say during the Oral Board Interview, how to pass the polygraph test, and what to say and what not to say to the psychologist conducting a pre-employment evaluation are examples. A question arises as to how accurate the psychological assessment is if candidates are being coached on what to say and what not to say during the selection process. This is unethical and dangerous; potentially resulting in hiring psychopaths to protect and serve society.

When comparing and contrasting personality traits of the police personality to that of domestic abusers, an interesting personality disorder known as "Psychopathy" also has similar characteristics. Characteristics of a psychopath that are similar to the police personality include the ability to manipulate, the need for stimulation, pathological lying, sense of entitlement, and a high rate of substance abuse. "Police officers suffer unusually high rates of alcoholism, being twice as likely as the general public to become problem drinkers (Constant, 1991)" (Boyce, 2006).

Substance abuse is also a contributing factor to domestic violence and is often seen in people with Antisocial Personality Disorder (APD, and Narcissistic Personality Disorder (NPD). A question arises to whether substance abuse among law enforcement is possibly related to the job as suggested in the literature, as a means to cope or self-medicate from negative stressors on the job; Or if it is a symptom of another disorder such as antisocial personality disorder or Psychopathy.

Since police officers are coached and schooled on the psychological testing; this poses a question as to the validity of the results since the answers are programmed responses by the evaluee rather than a genuine elicited response. Furthermore, it is easy for the psychopath to lie through the test and completely skew the results. Another question arises as to whether it is the coaching of police candidates or the police candidate already possesses psychopathological traits that enable them to pass the psychological instruments remains.

On the other hand, there are many well balanced police officers who are well suited for the position; however, it is those who engage in maladaptive behaviors such as domestic violence that this book will examine.

Psychological Test Instruments used in Police Selection

The following tests are used to determine personality traits and psychopathology among police candidates.

The MMPI-2

The MMPI-2 is a restandardized test from the original MMPI and is a common personality test instrument used in the selection process of police officers. The main objective of the MMPI-2 is to detect psychopathology. "The MMPI-2 uses standard (T) scores, which have a mean of 50 and a standard deviation of 10 and a T score greater than 65 on the MMPI-2 is considered clinically significant and therefore noteworthy" (Flieshman et. al., 2011).

Psychological testing among police candidates is to rule out candidates who would not otherwise make effective officers. In fact, "a T score greater than 65 on any of the MMPI-2 Basic Scales can be justifiably removed from the applicant pool" (Flieshman et. al, 2011).

The Personality Assessment Inventory (PAI)

The Personality Assessment Inventory, or PAI (Morey, 2007) is another psychological instrument used to measure psychopathology. "The PAI is composed of 344 questions as opposed to 567 items in the MMPI-2 and it is easier to read. Another feature of the PAI includes a 4-point scale for each item as opposed to a forced-choice true/false format as seen in

Police Personality and Domestic Violence

the MMPI-2" (Fleischer et. al., 2011).

Researchers have found that the Negative Impression (NIM) and Positive Impression (PIM) to be relevant to the police selection process. "Elevated NIM scores are modestly correlated with problem performance as a police officer after hire. These studies discovered that high NIM officers engaged in neglect of duty, made conduct mistakes, and were more likely than other officers to receive reprimands from supervisors" (Fleischer et.al., 2011); thus, justifying the exclusion from the applicant pool.

Additionally, the PAI clinical scales offer additional purposes for law enforcement selection. The PAI provides a scale to predict officer performance. This scale is called "The Antisocial (ANT) scale." "The Weiss et al. (2004) and Weiss et al. (2005) studies showed that the ANT full scale and its subscales (ANT-A/Antisocial Behaviors, ANT-E/Egocentricity, ANT-S/Stimulus Seeking) were associated with problem behaviors such as insubordination, excessive citizen complaints, neglect of duty, conduct mistakes, and termination for cause" (Fleischer et. al., 2011); thus, eliminating individuals with high T scores or >70.

Validity of the PAI

It is noteworthy to reveal that the prediction of personality disorders, substance abuse, and other maladaptive behaviors used in the selection process from scales and

Police Personality and Domestic Violence

measures do not provide peer-reviewed research to support the criterion of the PAI scales that measure of psychopathology. "Weiss, Hitchcock, et al. state that law enforcement candidates tend to produce profiles on self- report tests of psychopathology that have lower means than those found in normative samples, and very few individuals produce scale elevations" (Fleischer et. al., 2011). Self- reporting symptoms are biased and individuals with narcissistic psychopathy are convincing and have the ability to captivate others. They have the ability to distort reality and offer plausible alternative scenarios. This quality is attractive in the selection of law enforcement since thinking on their feet is a qualification of the job; thus, potentially skewing the results.

The California Psychological Inventory (CPI)

The California Psychological Inventory (CPI) is the second most widely used psychological instrument used in the pre-employment screening for police officers. The CPI offers 434 items and measures with 20 dimensions of personality over four major areas of personality: measures of poise, measures of normative orientation and values, measures of cognitive and intellectual functioning, and measures of role and interpersonal style" (Fliescher et. al, 2011). It is interesting to note that the CPI is popular within the law enforcement selection process and is not an instrument to be used to identify psychopathology but rather used for pre-employment purposes only. However,

Police Personality and Domestic Violence

the CPI is used in collaboration with other tests that do identify psychopathology such as the PAI and MMPI-2 (Fleischer et. al., 2011).

The Inwald Personality Inventory (IPI)

"The Inwald Personality Inventory (Inwald, 1982) contains 310-item true/false self-report inventory that focuses mainly on admitted past behavior patterns in an attempt to predict future job-related behaviors (Inwald, 2008)" (Fleischer et al., 2011). The test addresses the admission of past antisocial behaviors to which the evaluee will answer either true or false. "The IPI continues to be the most popular of the Inwald–Hilson measures for police psychological assessment (see, for example, Super, 2006)" (Fliescher et. al., 2011). Self-reporting of symptoms or past behaviors can be easily denied by the test taker; thus, skewing the results.

The Matrix-Predictive Uniform Law Enforcement Selection Evaluation Inventory (M-PULSE)

"The Matrix-Predictive Uniform Law Enforcement Selection Evaluation Inventory, commonly known as the M-PULSE (Davis & Rostow, 2008) is a 455-item inventory scored on a four-point scale that focuses primarily on identifying law enforcement officer candidates at risk for specific liabilities most frequently associated with performance problems as a law enforcement officer, such as criminal conduct" (Fleischer et. al, 2011). Additionally, the M-PULSE)

Police Personality and Domestic Violence

assesses for attitudes and other personality characteristics that may negatively impact police work; "Variables include Negative Self-Issues, Negative Perceptions Related to Law Enforcement, Unethical Behavior, and Unpredictability" (Fleischer et. al., 2011).

Procedural Methods used across the United States in the Selection of Police officers

A study performed by Cochrane et al revealed procedural methods that were used by police departments across the United States to determine the selection process of police officers. "Participants included personnel departments of municipal police agencies throughout the United States (Cochrane et al, 2008). "Municipal police departments were chosen because they are the most widely recognized law enforcement agencies and they represent the largest number of police or safety personnel in the United States" (Cochrane et al, 2008).

The researchers in this study randomly selected 355 municipal police agencies across the county out the 1200 current municipal police agencies in the United States and sent them a survey containing 20 questions regarding the selection procedures used by each individual agency. The random sample was selected based on geography and population size" (Cochran et al, 2008). Out of the 355 randomly selected agencies, 43% or155 agencies completed and returned the

Police Personality and Domestic Violence

surveys (Cochran et al, 2008). Agencies were further broken down into groups by size based on the population size served by the agency. "Departments were considered large if population size served was greater than 100,000, medium if between 25,000 and 100,000, and small if less than 25,000. The source used to select departments and determine population size was The National Directory of Law Enforcement Administrators and correctional Agencies (National Police Chiefs and Sheriffs Information Bureau, 1996)" (Cochran et al., 2008).

Table 1.1

"Types of Selection Procedures used in Police Departments before hiring a police officer by percentage" Cochrane et al 2009).

Municipal Police Agency Size

Procedure Type	Small =35	Medium 53	Large 67	Combined 155
Background Investigation	100.0	98.1	100.0	99.4
Medical exam	97.0	98.1	100.0	98.7
Interview	100.0	98.1	97.0	98.1
Application blank	97.0	90.5	98.5	95.5
Psychological assessment	73.5	94.3	98.5	91.6
Drug testing	70.5	90.5	95.5	88.4
Physical fitness	64.7	81.1	86.5	80.0
Polygraph	26.4	69.8	82.0	65.8
Civil Service Exam	32.3	50.9	56.7	49.7
Recommendation letters	50.0	35.8	53.7	46.5
Knowledge, skills, abilities	47.0	49.0	44.7	46.5
Other	26.4	31.3	27.7	20.5

Police Personality and Domestic Violence

Reliability and Validity

Reliability and validity of reported domestic violence appeared skewed in some studies as a result of suggesting that the studies revealed a high reliability and validity rate; however, at the same time, research also suggests that domestic violence is often under reported in the general population. The potential for the loss of the officer's job along with the Lautenberg Amendment provides additional barriers in reporting abuse and/or taking action against the officer. Therefore, it is suggested that the complex dynamics involved in police perpetrated domestic violence is underreported and may occur more frequently than what is actually reported.

"In a study by Aamodt et al revealed a metanalytic technique to determine whether law enforcement personal that engage in domestic violence and men in the general population batter have similar personality traits or disorders" (Aamodt et al, 2000). "The study revealed MMPI mean profiles of police officers and the batterer groups have almost no overlap.

On the validity scales with the exception of the L scale, and all of the clinical scales, the mean score of the batterers falls significantly higher than the mean score of the police officers" (Aamodt et al, 2000). "Additionally, validity scales revealed that men in the general population admitted having more deviant attitudes and behaviors than the police officers"

Police Personality and Domestic Violence

(Aamodt et al, 2000). The threats to the officer's job and livelihood are impacted if charged with the crime of domestic violence. Suggesting that some officers who perpetrate DV lied on the study questionnaire to protect their job.

It is interesting to note that on the K scale, batterers scored in the average range, whereas police officers scored much higher. This score may occur in truly well-adjusted persons with good ego strength. On the other hand, it may also occur in persons with some adjustment difficulties trying to present themselves more favorably, in employment situations (Aamodt et al, 2000). The results in this study are interesting since one of the first questions that arise when an officer is charged with domestic violence is how the officer fared on the pre-employment evaluation, which contains a battery of tests. Individuals who are masters at manipulation and deception may pass these tests. Furthermore, police officers who are skilled at manipulation and deception not only make effective officers, but utilize these tactics to abuse, coerce, intimidate, harass, hurt, manipulate their intimate partners and the criminal justice system.

Another study by Bergen et al stated "The probability of IPV-intimate partner violence in the police population can be applied to the national rates if the male police group constitutes a random sample of the larger population of adult males" (Bergen et al, 2000). Since police officers who batter

Police Personality and Domestic Violence

are within a sub-population of males who engage in domestic abuse; in addition to different variables that do not apply to both samples, along with different variables measured between the general population of males versus that of the sub-population of police officers who batter potentially refutes the statement by Bergen et al could prove false.

Furthermore, the pre-employment process, screening, measures of psychological instruments, background checks, overall intellectual functioning, police training and other tactics are carefully employed before the hiring process, in addition to ongoing training on the job. These batterers work within the very system where domestic violence laws are enforced; whereas domestic abusers within the general population may have previous histories of violence, and criminal histories that are not found within the police population.

There is also a police culture component that we will discuss later in the book, that impacts whether an officer will be charged with domestic violence. Many officers are protected by the what is known as the "blue wall" and they are rarely charged with the crime. However, things are changing, and police officers are being held accountable more now than ever.

A question arises as to whether the police profession, mental illness or personality disorder is responsible for the ability to manipulate and charm their way through the pre-screening process, in addition to having a higher intelligence

Police Personality and Domestic Violence

than that of males within the general public which may account for the difference in why police domestic violence is under reported. Or are these variables and traits similar?

MMPI MEAN T-SCORES FO R POLICE OFFICERS AND BATTERERS

A study performed by Aamodt et al set out to determine whether police officers as a group possessed personality characteristics that may predispose them to domestic violence. The researchers obtained data from two groups; police officers and batterers who were convicted of domestic violence. The information was obtained from individuals in these two comparison groups who had taken the MMPI. "The data was used to create the "police personality" and the "batterer personality" (Aamodt et al 2000).

The chart reveals that there are no overlaps. "On all of the validity scales with the exception of the L scale, and all of the clinical scales, the men score of the batterers falls significantly higher than the mean score of the police officers: (Aamodt et al, 2000).

Police Personality and Domestic Violence

Validity Scales and Interpretation

L Scale

Both groups scored within an average range.

F Scale

Batterers scored significantly higher and admitted to having more deviant attitudes and behaviors than of the police group. "In a valid profile, higher F scale scores correlate with increased psychopathology and also serve as a rough measure of the severity of the psychological distress experienced by the individual"(Aamodt et al., 2000).

Police officers scored within average range on the F scale. "People who score within this range are less likely to experience disabling psychopathology.

K Scale

Batterers scored within average range; suggesting opens in their self-description" (Aamodt et al, 2000).

Police officers scored within the average range; however their score fell significantly higher than that of the batterer's group. "This may suggest that the officers did not report as many symptoms as that of the batter group. In addition, this score may reveal that the officer is truly well rounded or that the police group was attempting present themselves more favorably" (Aamodt, 2000).

Police Personality and Domestic Violence

Clinical Scales Interpretation

On the clinical scales, police officers scored within average ranges, whereas the batter group scored significantly higher than that of the police officer group. In theory, "police officers may have scored within average range and did not exhibit any serious psychopathology. However, police officers may have had more motivation than batterers did to present themselves as "favorably." This theory is corroborated by the many coaching and training courses that officers engage prior to any pre-employment testing, interviews and so forth. These classes are designed so that the police officer will pass the pre-employment testing" (Aamodt et al, 2000).

Police Personality and Domestic Violence

Chapter Five

Police Culture and Training

Research has suggested that police culture plays a significant role in domestic violence perpetrated by police officers. Police culture has been in existence since its establishment in 1829 by Sir Robert Peel who launched the first paramilitary modeled police organization in London, establishing the London Police Department (Uchida 2010; Stevens 2008)" (Cochrane, 2008). "The paramilitary hierarchical chain of command intended to promote respect for authority, building camaraderie among those in uniform, and emphasizing ethical behavior from all officers would establish the foundation of police culture and influence that is still in existence today" (Uchida 2010; Black 1991) (Cochrane, 2011).

Solidarity among law enforcement has come to be known as "The Blue Wall" and is not only commonplace

Police Personality and Domestic Violence

among law enforcement but expected among the profession. The solidarity and strong sense of loyalty, lack of monitoring within the law enforcement culture; ultimately results in the police policing themselves. The lack of policies in place in addition to the absence of enforcement of laws and policies within law enforcement has made domestic violence among law enforcement difficult to challenge, treat, and resolve.

Research reveals the level of lethality involved in domestic violence by police officers as the most lethal form of domestic violence. This may be due to the accessibility of weapons and training. Additionally, police officers work within the very system where the victim will report the abuse and attempt to seek justice. The solidarity reaches far beyond the police department. It reaches into the judicial system where judges often side with the police officer.

Judicial bias is common among police officers who engage in domestic violence and charged with the crime. It is suggested that working within the same system, the criminal justice arena, members of that system also feel the same sense of loyalty, preventing victims from seeking necessary actions to protect themselves from the abuse, such as obtaining a personal protection order.

Personal protection orders are often denied by judges because of a federal law, The Lautenberg Amendment to the gun control act and family violence act (1968). This law prohibits any person convicted of domestic violence from possessing firearms, including a police officer "A law enforcement officer with such a conviction cannot carry a gun" (Allen, Hibler, & Miller 2000). This poses a significant threat to the officer's position since carrying a gun is part of the tools of the trade of police work. Other professions do not have the same threat of a potential loss of employment when charged with domestic violence.

Police culture also influences victim assistance and response to the domestic violence complaint. It is suggested that because of the officer's position and working within the criminal justice system where domestic violence is charged as a crime within the general population; is voided when the batterer is a police officer.

A lack of cooperation by the police department in prosecuting the police batterer, in addition to domestic violence that is often covered up due to police cultural influence, the police policing themselves, judicial bias, fear of liability within the police department and the Lautenberg amendment to the gun control act are all factors that are considered when charging a police officer with domestic violence. "In one study by Sgambelluri it is suggested that policing encourages and attracts individuals with characteristics associated with authoritarianism and many domestic abusers possess this same trait.

Police Personality and Domestic Violence

Although policing may enhance or influence attitudes and behaviors to abuse, in itself policing does not cause domestic violence. It is the attitudes, behaviors and police training that can further enhance an abuser's tactics on the victim" (Sgambelluri 2000).

Police Training and Tactics

Police training and tactics begin early on, as early as the pre-employment phase. Police officers are trained to tell the evaluating psychologist and the Oral Review Board exactly what they want to hear, and not what they would actually say if they were telling the truth. This poses a question as to whether police departments across the country are hiring genuine well-adjusted police officers who are suited for the police profession.

With appropriate coaching and training, police candidates are being passed off as "Competent" or fit for duty when these individuals may not be psychologically fit. "In studying domestic violence by police officers, it is important to determine whether the increased levels of domestic violence among law enforcement are due to characteristics of the individual officer; such as personality, background; conditions of the job itself or an interaction between the two" (Aamodt, 1998). Alternatively, research suggests that it is both individual personality traits along with police culture and training that constitute the police personality.

Police Personality and Domestic Violence

Common police training tactics used to perpetrate domestic violence by a police officer include utilizing departmental assets to harass, stalk, abuse, coerce or intimidate the victim, such as driving by the victim's house to let her/him know that they are watching them; utilizing databases to obtain information on the victim and the victim's friends and family; or putting taps on the phone of the victim; and utilizing other officers to further intimidate the victim and to cover-up misconduct. Other tactics include using physical control maneuvers that will not leave marks on the victim, arresting the victim, and twisting the truth to make the victim look crazy or like the problem.

Creative Report Writing 101

Police officers are responsible for writing police reports, and they know how to write a police report to their advantage to press charges against the victim. For those unfamiliar with domestic violence tactics used by police officers many may not believe a police officer could get away with doing this; however, it is a common tactic used in domestic violence by police officers or in excessive force cases. Police officers use this same tactic to write a police report to reflect a more different view of what actually happened when the officer or a fellow officer engages in police excessive force in an attempt to blame the excessive force as being necessary to subdue an alleged offender. This may be

Police Personality and Domestic Violence

true in some cases; however, it is also done to protect the officer, the department, and any liability that goes along with the excessive force injuries or misconduct, including domestic violence.

The victim turned into the "offender" narcis often surprised to see that the police report does not reflect the actual events that occurred. The same is true of police officers who engage in domestic violence and the police are called. Many times, fellow officers will go along with their co-worker, the off-duty officer who perpetrated the domestic violence that resulted in the police being called, and the officers who arrive at the scene will write the report to benefit their fellow colleague. This pattern is seen in the early example during the pre-employment testing phase, where officers scored higher on the K scale to present themselves more favorably. This trait is a form of manipulation, and deception which are commonly seen in individuals with psychopathy, and antisocial personality disorder, narcissistic personality disorder, and are also traits of domestic abusers. It should be noted that not all police officers will go along with the program when asked to write a false or embellished police report, and the officer will be arrested.

A more realistic scenario described by victims goes more like this: The police officer physically assaults the victim but doesn't leave any marks. The victim calls the police, and the police officer, the offender laughs at her telling her "who

Police Personality and Domestic Violence

do you think they'll believe you or me?" This infuriates the victim even more and the victim calls the police. The police arrive and when the victim tells her side of the story, the officers ask to see if there are any physical injuries. The victim lifts her shirt to show the officers only to realize that there aren't any marks, and if there are marks, they are lighter than the pain the victim feels. The offending officer tells his fellow officers "She was coming at me with a knife, what was I supposed to do let her stab me?" Then the victim is arrested for felonious assault. The victim becomes hysterical because of the lie the officer told. She never touched a knife. Then the police perpetrator says "She's also got mental health issues. Look at her. She can't control her emotions." The victim kicks and screams that she didn't do what he said she did, looking even more unhinged. When in reality she is fighting for her life, against a group of police officers who took the word of a fellow officer, while the victim is wrongfully arrested, physically, and psychologically abused, and given a tarnished reputation by her police batterer. Now she is facing criminal charges, along with being the victim of domestic violence. This scenario is very common and seen by many domestic violence agency and mental health counselors around the world.

Police officers, society, and juries will typically believe a police officer over an alleged offender most of the time. Juries often believe that an offender is making up stories to avoid incarceration or other punishment by the court. The above example was an actual domestic incident between an actual victim and her police officer boyfriend. It is also common for police batterers to twist the truth and turn the victim into the defendant.

Playing the Crazy Card

One of the most disturbing tactics among domestic violence by police officers is attempting to make the victim look crazy. Although this is common among all domestic abusers this tactic can have serious consequences for the victim. Common statements made by all domestic abusers in all populations may include: "She's crazy: she's bi-polar; she always does this on her period; she always acts like this once a month (referring to her menstrual cycle); she is emotionally unstable; I am worried about her, she has been acting very irrational lately; I'm not sure what to do anymore, I love her, but I can't take her mental instability; look at her, look how she is behaving" and so on.

Even more devastating and harmful to the victim is to have the victim psychiatrically evaluated under false pretenses. This is done when the abuser, a police officer, states that the victim, his intimate partner, has threatened to commit suicide or harm him. Fellow officers are then called to the house with a petition to have the victim taken to a psychiatric hospital. What makes this more devastating to the victim is that the hospital rarely questions a police petition. The hospital realizes that if a patient is brought in by the police, then they must be in severe distress.

According to Melton et al. "The jurisprudential basis of criminal law is the "police power," which authorizes the state to protect the community and to "ensure domestic tranquility. Civil commitment has traditionally been justified under the state's **parens patriae** authority to act as the "general guardian of all infants, idiots, and lunatics" (Melton et. al., 2007). In other words, the police have the power to have an individual committed to a psychiatric hospital under their discretion. They can use this power to abuse their power. This is one of the most common tactics used by police against their intimate partners (Melton et. al., 2007). Additionally, civil commitment states the terms describing the grounds for intervention such as mental disorder, a need for treatment, or is a threat to self or other. Police offices can and do write in their reports that their victim meets one of the criteria mentioned by making it appear as if it is the victim who is "mentally ill" or "mentally unstable."

A common scenario involves the victim being taken to the hospital in handcuffs by the very officers she has eaten dinner with at family gatherings. They are the friends of her batterer, a police officer. She is embarrassed, humiliated, confused, angry, and traumatized. When she arrives at the

Police Personality and Domestic Violence

hospital, the victim is rambling on trying to tell the nurse that she isn't crazy and that her husband is a police officer, and he did this to her. The victim is in extreme panic, her speech is pressured, she is crying hysterically. She is afraid at what will happen if they commit her. Everyone is afraid of the unknown, especially being admitted to a pysch unit of a hospital. The victim's attempt to plead with the hospital staff that she is not crazy while she is crying, yelling obscenities, and telling them the police did it only reinforces the police petition. The victim is in shock and her speech in incoherent as a result of the shock and the abuse.

The nurse will do the initial assessment and medication is often recommended to calm the victim down. In an actual case, the nurse began to give the victim an injection of an anti-psychotic, Haloperidol. The victim was aware of patient rights and the right to refuse treatment.

She refused the medication. The nurse was surprised at the patient's request. The patient asked why she was being given this drug and the nurse responded by telling the victim that the police report stated that she was bi-polar.

The victim was further traumatized. She had never had such a diagnosis; however, after this event, she was treated for Post-Traumatic Stress Disorder (PTSD) as a result of the emotional and physical abuse perpetrated by her police boyfriend.

This tactic has serious consequences on the victim's overall mental health, in addition to her overall credibility in the event that she has to call the police again for help.

The victim will be less likely to call the police for help in the future. This will have a significant impact on the power and control that the abuser has on the victim. He knows that she is afraid to call the police in the future because he tells her that her credibility is shot, and everyone already thinks she's crazy.

This tactic can also have serious consequences on the victim if she is going through a divorce and fighting for custody of the children. Any medical or legal document can have an impact on any situation and the police batterer understands this.

Police Personality and Domestic Violence

Chapter Six

Psychopathology and Domestic Violence

Various terms have been used to describe those who consistently exploit others and infringe society's rules for personal gain as a consequence of their personality traits, including antisocial personality disorder, sociopathy and psychopathy, or narcissistic personality disorder (NICE Clinical Guidelines, No. 77 National Collaborating Centre for Mental Health (UK). Leicester (UK): British Psychological Society; 2010). Criteria for Antisocial personality disorder (APD) These traits are seen in domestic abusers.

According to the DSM-5 APD diagnostic criteria includes the following:

A. A pervasive pattern of disregard for and violation of the rights of others, occurring since age 15 years, as indicated by three (or more) of the following:

Police Personality and Domestic Violence

1. Failure to conform to social norms with respect to lawful behaviors, as indicated by repeatedly performing acts that are grounds for arrest.
2. Deceitfulness, as indicated by repeatedly lying, use of aliases, or conning others for personal profit or pleasure.
3. Impulsivity or failure to plan ahead.
4. Irritability and aggressiveness, as indicated by repeated physical fights or assaults.
5. Reckless disregard for safety of self or others.

6. Consistent irresponsibility, as indicated by repeated failure to sustain consistent work behavior or honor financial obligations.
7. Lack of remorse, as indicated by being indifferent to or rationalizing having hurt, mistreated, or stolen from another.
B. The individual is at least age 18 years.
C. There is evidence of conduct disorder with onset before age 15 years.
D. The occurrence of antisocial behavior is not exclusively during the course of schizophrenia or bipolar disorder. (APA 2013).

In addition, according to the American Psychological Association (APA) The essential feature of antisocial personality disorder is a pervasive pattern of disregard for, and violation of, the rights of others that begins in childhood or early adolescence and continues into adulthood. This pattern has also been referred to as psychopathy, sociopathy, or dissocial personality disorder. Deceit and manipulation are central features in antisocial personality disorder. It is interesting to note that police officers use deceit and manipulation in police work to elicit confessions, or in undercover police work.

Personality traits among male domestic abusers include male privilege, sense of entitlement, a controlling and demanding demeanor, manipulative, deception, and authoritarianism, many of the same traits seen in the police personality. "Psychopathy has been one of the most powerful, if not the single most powerful predictor of continued violence across a variety of different samples including general criminal offenders of different crimes, including domestic violence, sex offenders, substance abusers, psychiatric patients, men and women, adolescents, and in various countries throughout the world" (Huss & Langhinrichsen-Rohling, 2006).

In a study performed by Huss & Langhinrichsen-Rohling revealed three typologies of batterers LLA: Low Level Antisocial, GVA: Generally Violent/Antisocial, BD: Borderline/Dysphoric, and FO: Family Only. "The study revealed a great deal of overlap between the Generally Violent, Antisocial (GVA) classification of batterers and many

Police Personality and Domestic Violence

dimensions of psychopathy" (2006). "Research has suggested that the generally violent/antisocial batterers (GVA) are characterized by general antisocial features and greater substance abuse, the most severe partner violence, and the commission of violence both against the partner and against others" (Huss & Langhinrichsen-Rohling, 2006).

This is an interesting finding and may be applied to police officers who batter. Police officers as a whole have a high rate of domestic violence, divorce and substance abuse. Past research has suggested that police related work and stressors may contribute to these findings. However, if this were the case, why do some officers engage in domestic violence whereas others do not? There appears to be a strong link to domestic violence, psychopathy and assessment for psychopathy should be at the forefront of the police selection process.

A psychological instrument, The Hare Psychopathy Checklist (PCL-R) relies on the truthfulness of responses. Psychopaths are notorious liars and part of the instrument includes third party interviews to include family members or other witnesses of the evaluee. Family members are bias and offer bias statements that will provide unreliable results. "Several studies assessing domestic violence perpetrators have relied on a self-reporting measure to assess psychopathy in their samples of male batterers; Yet the use of a self-reporting measure to assess psychopathy has been routinely criticized because a central feature of psychopaths is their ability to con and manipulate (Rogers, Vitacco, & Jackson, 2002)" (Huss & Langhinrichsen- Rohling, 2006).

"A study performed by and published by Campbell (1995) was based on a woman's belief that her partner might kill her. Certain terrorist tactics, such as choking to the point of the woman losing consciousness contribute to this belief" (Dutton & Kerry). "However, this belief notwithstanding, the personality disorder most likely to actually kill his spouse is dependent and passive- aggressive, not the profile predicted by these scales" (Dutton & A study by Showalter, Bonnie & Roddy (1980) concluded that, "especially significant was the fact that spousal killers lacked recorded histories of assaultive or other socially disturbing behavior" (Dutton & Kerry).

This is interesting in that we do not hear of police officers who abuse their intimate partners as in the example above until it is too late when the victim was murdered by the officer. It is then that it makes the news. A similarity includes police officers who batter, and psychopaths' alike do not always have past histories of abuse. For police officers, this may be due to departmental bias and cover up, and having the ability to manipulate, coerce, and deceive others; and with psychopaths they too have the ability to manipulate, coerce, charm and con others.

Police officers have the privilege and ability to take a life or liberty from individuals and when a psychopath has this authority and powerful privilege, they can easily turn it into misuse of power or abuses of authority in the hands of unethical, immoral individuals who do not regard the rights of others; a similar definition of antisocial personality disorder; and Psychopathy. These are traits and issues seen in police officers who batter and abuse their power.

Themes

Common themes emerged from the collected data included occupational stress related to police work as the most common cited material. Additionally, many of the studies performed included studies comparing large police departments versus smaller or rural police departments. These studies revealed that larger police departments had more exposure to critical incidents such as shootings and more action or negative stressors on the job as a potential for carrying over job related stress into the officer's family life, resulting in domestic violence.

On the other hand, other studies revealed a much different view of the problem to include individual personality traits of the officer, substance abuse, police training and tactics as variables responsible for domestic violence within the police population.

Both studies identified negative stressors related to

Police Personality and Domestic Violence

police work as potential risk factors to domestic violence within this population. "Another recurrent theme noted in the research relates to the effect that occupation has an impact on a person's perception and view of the world. For example, doctors, janitors, lawyers, and industrial workers develop distinctive ways of perceiving and responding to their environment. The same is true of police work. Elements in the police environment, danger, authority, and efficiency, as they combine to generate distinctive cognitive and behavioral responses in police: a "working personality" would be no different" (Skolnick).

It is also suggested that occupation tends to lead to lifestyle habits. For example, medical personal tends to be more health oriented due to their training and from what they see every day in the health care setting. Police work becomes a lifestyle and carried over into the home by overprotection of family members, suspicion and looking out for danger.

Patterns

Patterns in research included potential causes and risk factors for domestic violence to include police culture, police training and tactics learned in the profession, and individual personality traits to be the most commonly discussed among the literature.

Additionally, lack of policy, policing amongst themselves, and threat to the loss of job due to the Lautenberg

Amendment to the family violence act are components to protecting police officers who engage in domestic violence. Other classifications included demographic characteristics of the sample population including gender, rank of the officers, total years as a police officer, years on the job and how long the officer has been at present police department, age, marital status, surveys of victims and officers.

Gaps and Contradictions

Gaps and contradictions in the literature include a lack of empirical studies by the psychology profession, with a vast majority of the articles being published between 1990 through 1998. The decade long gap of articles relating to this sensitive topic ranges from 2000 to 2011 and my research has provided for very few articles on the topic. Limitations of scholarly sources, empirical data, research, and findings are significantly scarce during this time period. This may potentially be due to the emergence of police psychology becoming more recognized as an official discipline in the early 1990's during the same time when domestic violence awareness was still in its infancy.

Domestic violence by police officers is a special population of abuse and the dynamics of police culture, training, traits, and influence on family violence was addressed only within the law enforcement community during this time period; and still remains the constant today.

Police Personality and Domestic Violence

The explanations and theories of police officers who batter are vast and vary from context to context, including police stress and family spill over to be the most common theory. Additionally, research found that job burnout, constant negative stressors related to police work, emotional stress related to the job, critical incidences such as shootings, and substance abuse among the law enforcement community to be the most common variables and potential risk factors for committing domestic violence within the police family.

Other contradictions in research were broad. For example, authoritarianism and the need for power and control were common among police batterers. These traits are found in men who batter in the general public. Other abusive behaviors found in police officers and the general public includes economic abuse, sexual abuse, threats, intimidation, isolation, emotional abuse, using male privilege, and using the children as pawns in their sadistic abusive quest for power and control over their intimate partner, including encouraging parent alienation.

Other studies provide a look into the individual officer's personality traits through psychometric instruments that are used to recruit police officers and screen for the potential for "poor or weak" police officers. It is suggested that personality traits that make effective officers are also traits seen in men who batter in the general public.

Police Personality and Domestic Violence

For example, a study by Kraft states "The Inwald Personality Inventory (IPI) had slightly better predictive validity than the MMPI for forecasting and screening out potentially poor police recruits" (Kraft 2000). Police recruits are "weeded out" if they do not possess qualities that the department is looking for, such as a strong authoritative presence, strong ego, the ability to think quickly on their feet. Psychopaths have these same overlapping traits. Narcissistic psychopaths captivate judges, juries and audiences with the ability to offer plausible alternative scenarios no matter what the situation is. They think on their feet and provide believable explanations. Is this skill, training, or pathology?

Furthermore, White and Honig (1995) report a high incidence of domestic violence within law enforcement families, indicating that job characteristics such as "habituation to force, seeing force as a viable solution, rigid chain of command, expectation of compliance and the absence of outside input due to police solidarity enhance the risk for domestic violence even more (p. 200)" (Kraft, 2000).

Additionally, "the MMPI reveals new content scales, Butcher (1989) describes certain subscales capturing External Aggressive Tendencies including anger (measure of loss of control influenced by frustration or stress), high scores on a cynicism scale, antisocial practices and type-A behavior correlating with overbearingness aggressiveness, and overt directness" (Kraft, 2000) that may contribute to domestic violence by police officers.

Chapter Seven

Ethical Issues for the Psychology Professional

Ethical issues and dilemmas are vast in the area of police psychology as it relates to domestic violence within the police family. Ethical challenges may include identifying the client, Competence, adequate training, Confidentiality, Dual relationships, role conflict, boundary issues, and dealing with organizational demands.

Identifying the client

Identifying the client is one of the most challenging ethical issues for any psychology professional; yet it is even more challenging for the police psychologist or psychology professional who works with police officers who engage in domestic violence. Dual Relationships, Role Conflict and Boundary Issues are the most common ethical issues and pose a risk for the development of other ethical dilemmas.

Police Personality and Domestic Violence

Depending on the role that the forensic psychology professional is working will help in identifying the role that they will engage. For example, a psychologist who works for the police department on a regular basis may confer with investigators on a case; perform Fitness for Duty Evaluations (FFDE); in addition to administering in- service training to law enforcement personal within the department.

Furthermore, the psychologist working for a police department may be responsible for providing psychological services to all members of the police department including officers who may have attended or were engaged in previous services as mentioned above (Zelig, 1988).

Working as consultant, evaluator, and therapist within a police agency may cause conflict and boundary issues if the psychology professional is not cognizant of their role for each individual interaction.

A study performed by Zelig provided: "The ethical problems most often reported as ethical issues working as a police psychologist within a police department included confidentiality, dual relationships, and conflicts between the ethical standards of the psychologist and needs of the agency as the most commonly reported issues" (Zelig, 1988). "Principle 6 of the *Ethical Principles* addresses many of the concerns raised in this discussion: Psychologists respect the integrity and protect the welfare of the people and groups with whom they work. When conflicts of interest arise between clients and psychologists' employing institutions, psychologists clarify the nature and direction of their loyalties and responsibilities and keep all parties informed of their commitments" (APA, 1981).

Competence

Another issue found to contribute to ethical issues in police personality, police psychology and domestic violence includes the scarce amount of evidenced based practice regarding this topic. Competence is not only required to do any job, but it is also an ethical obligation of the psychology professional. "According to the APA Code of Ethics "Psychologists undertake ongoing efforts to develop and maintain their competence. 2.04 *Bases for Scientific and Professional Judgments* Psychologists' work is based on established scientific and professional knowledge of the discipline" (APA, 1981).

The lack of scientific evidenced based practice and lack of information and training puts the psychologist and the client in a precarious position; potentially resulting in harming the client. The psychologist may turn to the police agency for information to better understand the nature of the problem. Asking for guidance from the police organization to obtain information and knowledge about police topics, such as domestic violence by police officers to help the psychology professional to perform their job may potentially result in bias on behalf of the department and individual officer inquired about. This act could potentially harm the victim, individual officer, or department.

According to the Specialty Guidelines for Forensic Psychology 4.01 Scope of Competence states "Forensic psychologists provide competent services to clients and other recipients of forensic services in a manner consistent with the profession. Competent provision of services includes the psychological and legal knowledge, skill, thoroughness and preparation reasonably necessary for the provision of those services" (APA, 1991). "In addition, the scope of competence encourages forensic psychologists to consult with other psychology professionals to establish competence in the area in question" (APA, 1991).

Adequate training

Adequate training and competence go hand in hand. Information on domestic violence by police officers is scarce. It is vital for the psychology professional to familiarize themselves in police issues, culture, dynamics of domestic violence and how it relates to the individual person or situation to provide an accurate assessment. The psychologist should always follow ethical guidelines provided by the APA, be aware of research in the field, be knowledgeable about applicable laws, including jurisdictional, federal, state, and case law that may impact Practice" (McCutheon, 2000).

Furthermore, it is important for the psychologist to use the most up to date information in the field. A key component in addressing the issue of maladaptive police behaviors, including police officers who engage in domestic violence begins with understanding the cultural influences involved.

Additionally, another key component comprises of lack of departmental policy when an officer engages in domestic violence. Only three states in the country have approved a law to mandate that all police departments within the state have a department policy on domestic violence by police officers. The International Association of Chiefs of Police (IACP) has developed a model policy for departments to utilize in helping them to design such policy; however, it should be noted that it is only a model policy. It requires laws to be passed to force departments to design an internal policy for their department.

This poses yet another problem; the police are designing individual departmental policies to police their own. This causes great bias and issues for victims and the community; in addition to putting the psychologist in a precarious position with no laws to guide them on the issue. The internal departmental policies are typically designed to protect the individual officer and the police agency to which the officer works.

Police Personality and Domestic Violence

Domestic violence by police officer's is still considered to be in its infancy making it challenging for the psychology professional to prevent role confusion.

Confidentiality

Confidentiality and identification of the client is paramount when working as a forensic psychology professional. Depending on the psycholegal question will help in identifying who the client is. According to Zelig "This problem is often embedded in the context of mandatory referrals in which a police officer is required to see a psychologist for treatment and/or evaluation.

These occasions usually occur when an officer's fitness for duty is questioned, when the officer is involved in a traumatic or critical incident, such as shooting a criminal suspect or being shot themselves; or when the police administration desires information about an officer's psychological status so that the most appropriate disciplinary action can be taken in cases of misconduct" (Zelig, 1988).

Since domestic violence affects the officer, the victim, and the community, ethical obligations can easily become blurred. When a police officer commits domestic violence, the community loses trust in the officer. Additionally, the community may lose trust in the police department if the department does not handle the incident appropriately.

There are many factors as to the ethical obligations of

the agency, the officer, and the psychology professional. "In all these instances, confidentiality between the officer and the psychologist is at most limited and often nonexistent. Therefore, it may not be in the officer's best interest to reveal certain information. At the same time, this information may be valuable to the police administration (and the community secondarily) in deciding whether to retain, suspend, terminate, or change the work assignment of an impaired or traumatized officer" (Zelig, 1988), including officers charged with crimes such as domestic violence.

Another issue arising from confidentiality and ethical issues is duty to warn and dangerousness. "These concerns arise in police populations, not as the result of high rates of psychopathology, but because of an officer's high exposure to what Monahan (1981) described as environmental correlates of violent behavior such as the immediate availability of weapons and potential victims. Many officers of course, frequently encounter antagonistic and violent citizens who could provoke an inappropriate response from an officer whose controls and inhibitions are compromised" (Zelig, 1988).

Dealing with Organizational Demands

Organizational demands are another issue faced by police and forensic psychologists. "There are times when the administration asked the psychologist to perform psychological evaluations on officers and to change the results

Police Personality and Domestic Violence

if the police administration did not like the outcome. Presumably, this was done so that the psychological evaluation could support the police administration's desire regarding the officer's position; either to protect or remove the officer from their duties" (Zelig, 1988). Other issues include asking the psychologist to perform psychological evaluations when learning that an officer is taking medication such as Prozac for depression.

The Specialty Guidelines for Forensic Psychologist 9.02 Conflicts with Organizational Demands states "If the demands of an organization with which a forensic psychologist is affiliated or for whom they are working conflict with the Guidelines, the forensic psychologist clarifies the nature of the conflict, makes known the recommendations of the Guidelines, and to the extent feasible, resolves the conflict in a way consistent with the Guidelines" (APA, 1991).

Ethical principles are put in place as a guideline to protect both the client and psychology professional from harm, and to guide them in delivering non-partisan, culturally sensitive care with clarity and objectivity. The research has identified all ethical principles as potential dilemmas. The ethical principles of beneficence, nonmalfeasance, autonomy and justice are identified throughout the literature.

According to the Specialty Guidelines for Forensic

Psychologists 2.01.01 Impartiality states "When offering expert opinion to be relied upon by a decision maker, teaching, or conducting research, the forensic psychologist embraces nonpartisanship and demonstrates commitment to the goals of accuracy, objectivity, fairness, and independence. The forensic psychologist treats all participants and weighs all data, opinion, and rival hypotheses impartially" (APA, 1991).

Beneficence and Nonmaleficence

Beneficence and Nonmaleficence go hand in hand. Beneficence is the promotion of good. This principle reinforces promoting actions to clients that will benefit them in making the best decision for them by weighing all available options. The option with the least possible harm should be taken (APA 2010). It should be noted that the client to which the forensic psychology professional serves is not the only persons or entities that the psychology professional is responsible to. Integrity is a foundational responsibility of the psychology professional. "Forensic psychologists hold trust relationships with clients, legal representatives, courts, all other participants in forensic matters, professional bodies, and society. These trust relationships can be put at risk by lack of integrity, lack of responsibility, lack of respect, or conflicts of interest that may compromise independence, objectivity, or other professional responsibilities" (APA, 1991).

An example of beneficence in domestic violence by

police officers as it relates to police personality may result in a bias opinion by the psychology professional. For example, if the psychology professional is performing a fitness for duty evaluation on a police officer and the psychologist has been a victim of domestic violence; in addition to understanding that police officers tend to be authoritative by nature and "stick to together" the opinion of the psychologist may become skewed as a result of personal and professional experience and bias.

The psychology professional should always treat every individual as a new case and not fall into generalizing the police population. For example, a police officer may have PTSD as a result of a critical incident on the job, such as a shooting (being shot or shooting a suspect) and is exhibiting difficulty coping that resulted in domestic violence. The officer may engage in substance abuse and aggression both on and off the job (common among the PTSD population).

If the psychologist is not objective and assumes that the officer is a batterer and does not considered the cause or motive behind the officer's maladaptive behaviors the psychologist may recommend that the officer is not fit for duty as a result of battering traits. This would cause harm to the officer, potentially losing their position as a police officer.

If the officer engages in family violence as a symptom of aggression from PTSD symptoms and inability to cope; then the officer should be offered an opportunity for rehabilitation.

Police Personality and Domestic Violence

A diagnosis of PTSD is not an excuse for family violence; however, research has revealed a high rate of aggression and family conflict within the PTSD population of clients.

Nonmaleficence is the bioethical principle promoting "to do no harm." This is a fundamental principle in psychology. To avoid potential ethical conflicts or violations, the forensic psychologist should weigh potential outcomes when evaluating risks versus benefits in each individual client. "Because psychologists' scientific and professional judgments and actions may affect the lives of others, they are alert to and guard against personal, financial, social, organizational, or political factors that might lead to misuse of their influence. Psychologists strive to be aware of the possible effect of their own physical and mental health on their ability to help those with whom they work" (APA, 2010).

The criminal justice system is an adversarial arena and working with law enforcement takes on a whole new set of potential ethical issues. Police officers are often considered "To be the law;" they represent the law. Many individuals are intimidated by the mere presence of a police officer and society is conditioned to respect authority and the police profession.

Police officers are trained to elicit the response they want to hear. They are trained in twisting the truth to elicit confessions and this training technique is often spilled over into other areas of their lives. It is essential that the forensic

Police Personality and Domestic Violence

psychologist to remain objective and not get caught up in the partisanship of doing what an individual officer or agency expects from them if it is not within the scope of professional standards and practice.

Police officers are trained to manipulate outcomes, elicit information in a way that the psychologist is agreeing with the officer. The psychologist should be vigilant to interrogation and interview techniques used by police officers to avoid falling into this trap. The psychologist could potentially be viewed as a "Gun for hire" if they do not remain objective. This would not only hurt the client, but the reputation of the forensic psychologist that may also include sanctions from the state board. (APA 2010).

Autonomy

It is important for the psychologist to allow the officer to exercise their autonomy; however, it is suggested that police culture, training, along with police personality traits changes a police officer's overall persona, individuality and sense of autonomy. Autonomy is one of the bioethical principal's that promotes the sense of "self" when making independent, individual choices and decisions regarding their care.

The issue of role conflict and confidentiality are concerns. For example, a police officer who is undergoing an FFDE will most likely be resistant to telling the truth in fear of losing their job. Additionally, police officers are trained to skillfully deceive suspects to elicit confessions and this tactic is carried over into psychiatric evaluations with the psychologist. The psychologist can help the officer in attaining their individual autonomy by offering honest, clear, detailed information regarding evaluation, care, treatment planning and legal situation.

Justice

Finally, the research reveals that the ethical principal "Justice" refers to Justice is the principle that promotes the moral rightness, fairness, or equity of the client. The psychology professional can promote this principle by affording the client resources and opportunity to receive medical and mental health services. Each client is unique and will require a unique treatment plan designed around their individual needs.

As mentioned earlier, an ethical issue that arises in the research of domestic violence by police officers is a legal factor concerns a federal law; the Lautenberg amendment to the Gun Control Act of 1968 (Family Violence act) prohibits any person convicted of domestic violence from possessing firearms. A law enforcement officer with such a conviction cannot carry a gun" (Allen, Hibler, & Miller 2000). This poses a significant problem for the officer because carrying and using firearms are part of the tools needed to do the job of a police officer. The officer's personal life and professional life collide

Police Personality and Domestic Violence

making it difficult to treat the problem of domestic violence by law enforcement.

The psychologist may fall into the same trap as other members of the judicial system, such as the judge when determining fitness for duty, or other decisions that may impact the officer. The psychologist my feel guilty about the officer potentially losing their job and livelihood threatened. They may fear retaliation by the individual officer or other members of law enforcement due to the solidarity of the force and the emotions of the psychologist may guide their decision. This would be a great injustice to all who the psychologist is responsible.

Appreciation of individual differences is another responsibility of the psychology professional. "When Interpreting assessment results, including clinical and automated interpretations, the psychologist takes into account the purpose of the assessment of the person being assessed, including situational, personal, linguistic, and cultural differences, that might affect the psychologist's judgments or reduce the accuracy of their interpretations, and they identify any significant strengths and limitations of their procedures and interpretations" (APA, 1991). This ethical obligation may reinforce the potential fear of confusion on behalf of the psychologist due to taking cultural influence into consideration. The Psychologist must remember that they are not taking away the police officer's position if they are ultimately convicted of domestic violence; but rather it is the responsibility and act by the police officer who engaged in the act of DV.

Chapter Eight

Further Research

When domestic violence is committed by a law enforcement officer, unique challenges and barriers to reporting the abuse and seeking safety become a central theme for victims. Rehabilitation for the perpetrator is limited when the police officer is constantly guarded by the police department, in addition to lack of accountability for the officer's actions, lack of enforcement of laws by the department, and judicial bias, all play a role in managing domestic violence by police.

Further research and available forensic services are needed in this area of study. Monitoring police officers both on and off the job to identify whether there is a link between police work and family spillover can also be done through new research and research design for future researchers on the topic.

Moreover, due to the lack of information on the psychology behind police officers who batter provides a disadvantage to the mental health community in providing potential solutions, interventions and strategies in addressing the scope of the problem.

Collaboration among law enforcement, the mental health and health care system, the criminal justice system and the community need to work in concert with one another to address domestic violence within the police family.

Evaluations, psychological instruments, providing fitness for duty exams regularly, and monitoring officers for job related stress is suggested in both identifying problem officers and those who may be affected by police work whereby their perception becomes skewed potentially resulting in family violence.

Finally, lack of current information, lack of disciplinary action by the department taken when an officer abuses his intimate partner, lack of resources for victims of police perpetrated domestic violence (PPDV) and bringing awareness on this very sensitive topic should be at the forefront.

Each department is responsible in policing their own officers who abuse their power. Individual discretion within the department causes inconsistent delivery of sanctions against officers and lack of resources and safety for victims. However, with the increase in community awareness, activists and

Police Personality and Domestic Violence

society are holding officers accountable more now than ever. This has led four States to develop model policies on domestic violence that have been developed only over the past couple of years with the most recent being Florida State.

Moreover, gaps in research and other deficiencies in the availability of data can have a significant impact on the researcher, victim assistant providers, and medical and mental health providers in providing interventions and prevention strategies to combat the problem and accommodate the needs of both police officers and victim.

More than 80 years ago a man by the name of August Vollmer advocated for policy development within the police agency designed to allow only the most qualified, ethically grounded individuals to serve as police officers. Vollmer was the first to introduce the use of psychological and intelligence testing into the recruitment process (Vollmer 1921:571) (Cochrane et al, 2008). Policy development can be enhanced as we learn more about policing, and the issues that arise from officer involved incidents.

Additionally, policy reform will be limited without further research. The research topic influences society, victims, liability for police departments, and restricts further researcher for future scholars. Without quality scholarly sources and availability of research on this topic, we are allowing a problem to continue without resolve.

Police Personality and Domestic Violence

Chapter Nine

Interventions

Safety First

Regardless of cultural influence or threat to the officer's job, a victim's safety is the first intervention in domestic violence. Research has revealed a high rate of homicide-suicide involving domestic violence among the police profession. This may be due to the accessibility to weapons within law enforcement.

Although the solidarity among police has been evident since its existence, the law enforcement community should be enforcing solidarity and integrity as one. Protecting fellow officers who engage in domestic violence not only tarnishes the reputation for the law enforcement community, but fellow officers are ending their lives and the lives of their loved ones through homicide/suicide. In the end, the officers are not protecting their fellow officer, but helping them to commit a crime and potentially ending the life of the victim and the fellow officer.

Zero Tolerance Policy

A zero-tolerance policy should be enacted by all police departments. In addition, the development of domestic violence policy within the police department is needed to guide officers in handling domestic calls and understanding procedures and protocols when one of their own is charged with domestic violence. Many times, officers do not know what to do if an officer within their department has engaged in domestic violence; leaving it up to each individual officer's discretion on whether to arrest the officer or look the other way.

Education

Domestic violence calls within the general public are among the most dangerous for police officers. For this reason, police officers are educated in the dynamics of domestic violence, psychology of the victim and perpetrator to increase safety for the officer. The police officer who batters takes advantage of this knowledge and uses it against the victim to further intimidate, harass, coerce, and terrorize. This is an example of the police batterer utilizing police training to further abuse the victim.

Educating law enforcement personnel on domestic violence is an obligation, and it begins in the police academy. In fact, one of the questions on the oral review board during the pre-employment exam includes this question "If your partner was caught doing……How would you respond?" and the police candidate gives the obvious answer…. "I would report it to my supervisor." But, in the real world this does not always happen. Therefore, the police academy is the perfect place to begin education on domestic violence policy and training.

It is also important to understand how the stressors of police work can affect police officers. Police officers without psychopathological personality traits may engage in domestic violence as a result of negative stressors seen in police work; therefore, it is vital for officers to understand their "triggers" or when they are exhibiting signs of stress that begin to affect their overall well-being, sleep pattern, eating pattern, anxiety level, and relationships. This does not excuse the officer's actions, but it can shed light on the officer's behavior if they self-evaluate their feelings and behaviors.

Healthy Lifestyles

Another suggestion in the prevention of domestic violence among law enforcement is monitoring officers for occupational stress, offering family assistance, and providing routine psychiatric evaluations. Police work is not only stressful and can be dangerous, but it can also result in

Police Personality and Domestic Violence

posttraumatic stress disorder (PTSD) due to critical incidents or constant negative stressors. PTSD is linked to anger outbursts, aggression, and substance use. These behaviors can lead to lashing out violently on the job and in the officer's personal life.

Healthy lifestyles should be part of law enforcement education, beginning in the police academy, and throughout the officer's career. Understanding individual limitations and stress levels will help to prevent anger outbursts directed at citizens and in the officer's personal life.

Promoting a healthy diet, exercise, and overall balance for well-being is recommended. A healthy balance includes physical, emotional/psychological, occupational, social, spiritual, and intellectual well-being in promoting healthy lifestyles.

Chapter Ten

Breaking the Silence

Probably one of the most difficult suggestions is to ask a police officer to break the silence among what is known as "The Blue Wall." The blue wall is a result of the solidarity among law enforcement. From the very beginning police officers are taught to "have each other's backs" not only in the field but off duty. Research has found that the unity among law enforcement goes beyond the job and many officers feel obligated to protect their fellow officer even when they are aware of wrongdoing. This is an area that needs to be addressed and enforced by the law enforcement community. There are many reasons and theories for this.

For example,

1. It is suggested that officers have each other's backs both on and off duty because one day that officer may have to protect

Police Personality and Domestic Violence

or save that officers life one day.

2. The liability of the police agency has a lot to lose when it comes to abuses of power. Therefore, agencies will embellish, and create false police reports to match what reporting officers will say in a court of law. This tactic is done to protect the police agencies reputation, and credibility with the criminal justice system, and the community.

Breaking the silence is complex. It is asking individual officers and police agencies to break "the code" that has been enforced for centuries. It will take time, education, awareness, and policy change to help break the code of silence and to bring justice to those who abuse their power in the name of the badge.

With social media, and new training at police academies and police agencies, the police agencies and officers are breaking that code by informing other officers who break the law, that they are not going to jail because of their crime and refuse to lie for fellow officers.

Discussing scenarios relating to receiving, arriving on the scene, and dealing with domestic violence calls, and learning that the perpetrator is one of their own is an area of training and education that should be rehearsed over and over. This will help officers who are uncomfortable dealing with a colleague committing a crime.

Police Personality and Domestic Violence

Individual Psychotherapy and Monitoring

The criminal justice system has recommended anger management as an intervention measure among domestic batterers. The foundation of domestic violence is not about anger, it is about power and control. Domestic violence continues to grow in epidemic proportion because of a lack of knowledge and interventions on the topic. Anger is a result of a loss of control, and anger management can aid the abuser in alternatives to violence; however, it is the underlying psychopathology of the individual officer that should be reviewed.

Additionally, everyone is unique and will deal with stress in different ways; therefore, individual personality, circumstances, years on the police force, personal coping skills, support systems, the magnitude of the stressful events, overall occupational duties, and uniqueness of the police organization will all have an impact on the individuals overall stress levels and well- being.

In addition to these factors, interventions and treating the police batterer should include an individualistic approach to include the individual officer's biopsychosocial makeup, physical condition, disability (if applicable), mental health, medications (if any), an understanding of the officers current coping skills, and cultural beliefs and attitudes including police culture and attitudes should be examined when developing treatment plans, or whether to keep the officer on the force after receiving reports of excessive force or domestic violence.

Leadership

Leadership within the police agency has a significant impact on the integrity of the agency. This integrity is felt throughout the police department. An agency with high integrity is an agency with a moral honest leader. The strong morals and honesty demonstrated by a leader with integrity will reinforce the agency's mission statement and the community's expectations of professional policing. An agency with integrity will have community trust. "Power and authority are tools that law enforcement must use judiciously and ethically" (McCartney & Parent 2012). Without ethical standards, this power can be misused.

Good leadership will not tolerate domestic violence perpetrated by police officers. However, police chiefs who are batterer's themselves, or fellow officers who view domestic violence negatively will tend to side with their coworker. This dynamic has a significant impact on victim assistance, and on whether the officer will be charged with the crime of domestic violence. Research suggests that corrupt agencies begin at the top. Agencies with leaders of high moral code will weed out problem officers and will not tolerate officers covering up crimes, including domestic violence. These leaders train their officers to uphold a high moral code and to follow agency

Police Personality and Domestic Violence

protocol and the law enforcement oath.

Conclusion

Domestic violence by police officers remains a pervasive problem within society and among the law enforcement community. The literature has revealed that individual personality traits, the lack of empirical evidenced based practice and coaching before and during pre-employment evaluations offers skewed and invalid data to the psychology and law enforcement community.

Skewed results and questions remain as to whether police officers are being hired as a result of being among those who have not been "weeded out" among the selection process and are among the truly "good officers" who are victims of occupational stress and hazards; or are psychopaths who have conned their way through the system remains in question.

Dr. Frank Ochberg shares the opinion of many psychology experts. He believes that psychopaths, a term often used interchangeably with antisocial personality disorder (APD) are human predators with absolutely no empathy for others, no desire to conform to social norms. It is suggested that psychopaths have no conscious and psychopathy has nothing to do with being out of touch with reality or being psychotic. These individuals are responsible for their deeds and wrong doings. He also believes that the only treatment for

Police Personality and Domestic Violence

psychopaths is to catch them and to convict them and to let them age in isolation.

He also states that there are psychology professionals who claim that they have been successful in behavioral modification or psychoanalysis; however, Dr. Ochberg believes that applying the usual psychiatric and psychological techniques only makes a psychopath a better psychopath. Psychopaths learn to fool others; how to pretend to have feelings of concern in order to get what they want and to appease the criminal justice system.

Community awareness, education, breaking the silence among victims, their families, and within the law enforcement community will aid in the reduction and prevalence of domestic violence by police officers.

Community awareness is a powerful tool, and social media has played a significant role in bringing awareness to this sensitive issue and in exposing police officers who abuse their power. The use of cameras has made this possible. More police officers are being held accountable for their actions today than in the past.

Additionally, individual psychotherapy can support the perpetrator in gaining new behavioral concepts such as their need to control and believe that the world is an unsafe place as a result of the profession can help in the suspicion that police officers are often faced with. Finally, cooperation from the

Police Personality and Domestic Violence

police administration, breaking the code of silence and solidarity among the profession, availability of resources for the victim, and community awareness will serve to reduce and expectantly cease domestic violence by police offices.

Police Personality and Domestic Violence

Reference

Aamodt, m., Brewster, J., Raynes, B. (2000) *Is the Police Personality Predisposed to Domestic Violence?* Domestic Violence by Police Officers; Compilation of Papers. 15-20. FBI Academy: Quantico

Anderson, A., Celia, Lo. (2010). Intimate Partner Violence within Law Enforcement Families. *Journal of Interpersonal Violence*, 26 (6). 1176-1193. doi: 10.1177/0886260510368156

Anderson, G., Litzenberger, R., Plecas, D. (2002) "Physical evidence of police officer stress", *Policing: An International Journal of Police Strategies & Management*, 25 (2) 399 – 420

Bartol, C.R. & Bartol, A.M. (2008). *Criminal behavior. A psycholsocial approach* (Eighth ed.). Upper Saddle River, NJ, USA: Pearson Prentice Hall.

Bergen, G., Bourne-Lindamood, C., Brecknock. S. (2000). *Incidence of Domestic Violence Among Rural and Small Town Law Enforcement Officers.* Domestic Violence by Police Officers; Compilation of Papers. 63-73. FBI Behavioral Science Unit. Quantico.

Cochrane, R., Tett, R., Vandecreek, L. (2008) Psychological Testing and the Selection of Police Officers; A National Survey. *Criminal Justice and Behavior*, 30 (5), 511–537.

D'Angelo, J. (2000). Addicted to Violence: The Cycle of Domestic Abuse Committed by Police Officers. Retrieved from: *Domestic Violence by Police Officers; Compilation of Papers.* 149-162. FBI Academy: Quantico.

DeCrescenzo, D. (2005). Early Detection of the Problem Officer. *FBI Law Enforcement Bulletin.* 74 (7) pg15-18. Retrieved from the FBI Resource Center.

Diagnostic and statistical manual of mental disorders. Text revision. DSM-IV-TR (Fourth ed.). (2000). Arlington, VA, USA: American Psychiatric Association.

Dutton, D., Kerry, G. Modus Operandi and Personality Disorder in Incarcerated Spousal Killers. Retrieved from

Police Personality and Domestic Violence

Erwin, J. M., Gershon, R. M., Tiburzi, M., Lin, S. (2005). Reports of Intimate Partner Violence Made Against Police Officers. Journal of Family Violence, 20 February, 2005.

Fleishman, E., Cleveland, J., Kitaeff, J., (2011) Handbook of Police Psychology; Series in Applied Psychology: Routledge.

Gaines, J., Jermier, J. (1983) Emotional Exhaustion in a High Stress Organization. *The Academy of Management Journal,* 26 (4) 567-586.

Hall, C. S., & Lindzey, G. (1957). *Theories of personality.* New York, NY: John Wiley & Sons.

Huss, M. and Langhinrichsen-Rohling, J. (2007) Assessing the Generalization of Psychopathy in a Clinical Sample of Domestic Violence Perpetrators. *Law and Human Behavior*

Huss, M., Langhinrichsen-Rohling, J. (2006) Assessing the Generalization of Psychopathy in a Clinical Sample of Domestic Violence Perpetrators. Journal of Law and Hum Behavior

International Association of Chiefs of Police (2003) Domestic Violence by Police Officers; A Policy of the IACP; Police Response to Violence Against Women Project

Janik, J., Kravitz, H. (2010). Linking Work and Domestic Problems with Police Suicide. *Suicide and Life-Threatening Behavior,* 24 (3), 267–274. Fall 1994.

Johnson, Boulin, L., Todd, M., Subramanian, G. (2005). Violence in Police Families: Work-Family Spillover. *Journal of Family Violence,* 20 (1)

Klein, R., Klein C. (2000).The Extent of Domestic Violence within Law Enforcement: An Empirical Study. Retrieved from: *Domestic Violence by Police Officers.pg.* 225-232. FBI Academy: Quantico.

Kraft, K. (2000). Violence Risk Assessment for Police Force Families. The Psychiatric Institute of Washington. Retrieved from: *Domestic Violence by Police Officers; Compilation of papers* pg. 233-243. FBI Academy: Quantico.

Luyten, P., Blatt, S. (2011). Integrating theory-driven and empirically-

Police Personality and Domestic Violence

derived models of personality development and psychopathology: A proposal for DSM V. Clinical Psychology Review 31 (2011) 52–68

Mayer, J. D. (2005). A classification of DSM-IV-TR mental disorders according to their relation to the personality system. In J. C. Thomas & D. L. Segal (Eds.), *Comprehensive handbook of personality and psychopathology (CHOPP) Vol. 1: Personality and everyday functioning*. New York, NY: John Wiley & Sons.

Melton, G.B., Petrila, J., Poythress, N.G., Slobogin, C. (1997). *Psychological evaluations for the courts. A handbook for mental health professionals and lawyers* (Second ed.). New York, New York, USA: The Guilford Press.

Miller, C., Barrett, G. (2008). The Coachability and Fakability of Personality-Based Selection Tests Used for Police Selection. *Public Personnel Management;* 37 (3): pg. 339

Mullins, W., McMains, M.J. (2000). Impact of Traumatic Stress on Domestic Violence in Policing. Retrieved from: *Domestic Violence by Police Officers; Compilation of papers* pg. 247-268. FBI Academy: Quantico.

Munaker, J. (2010). Investigating Domestic Abuse: Law Enforcement's Role in Homicide   Prevention and Ending Intergenerational Violence LE Training Curriculu. *Retrieved from Google Scholar: Violence Against Women; United States Department of Justice.*

Nicoletti, J., Spencer-Thomas, N. (2000). A Cognitive Processing Model for Assessing and Treating Domestic Violence and Stalking by Law Enforcement Officers. *Domestic Violence by Police Officers; Compilation of papers* pg. 269-284. FBI Academy: Quantico.

Oeheme, K., Martin, A. (2011) A practical plan for prevention and intervention: Florida's new Model Policy on officer-involved domestic violence

Sgambelluri, R., (2000)/ *Police Culture, Police Training, and Police Administration: Their Impact on Violence in Police Families.* Domestic Violence by Police Officers; Compilation of Papers. 309-322. FBI Academy: Quantico.

Shockey-Eckles, M. (2011). Police Culture and the Perpetuation of the Officer Shuffle: The Paradox of Life Behind "The Blue Wall". Humanity & Society, 35, 290-309. Argosy University Library

Police Personality and Domestic Violence

Online Proquest database

Quinn, V. (2000). Training Approaches for the Prevention of Officer-Involved Domestic Violence. Domestic Violence Self-Assessment Tool for Law Enforcement. *Domestic Violence by Police Officers; Compilation of papers* pg. 285-296. FBI Academy: Quantico.

Sgambelluri, R., (2000)/ Police Culture, Police Training, and Police Administration: Their Impact on Violence in Police Families. *Domestic Violence by Police Officers; Compilation of papers* pg. 309-322. FBI Academy: Quantico.

Shannon, L., Walker, R. 92006). Police Attitudes Toward Domestic Violence Offenders. Journal of Interpersonal Violence, 21 (10), 1365-1374.

Sheehan, D. (2000). Domestic Violence by Police Officers: A compilation of papers submitted to the Domestic Violence by Police Officers Conference at the FBI Academy: Quantico.

Warren, H. C., & Carmichael, L., *Elements of human psychology* (Rev. Ed.; Boston, MA: Houghton Mifflin, 1930), p. 333/Cited in Allport, *Pattern & growth in personality* (1937/1961, p.36).

Weiss, R., Weiss, W. (2010) Criterion-Related Validity in Police Psychological Evaluations

Young, A.T., Fuller, J., Riley, B. (2008). On-Scene Mental Health Counseling Provided Through Police Departments. *Journal of Mental Health Counseling,* 30 (4) 345-361.

Police Personality and Domestic Violence

www.ingramcontent.com/pod-product-compliance
Lightning Source LLC
Chambersburg PA
CBHW072337290526
45794CB00002B/910